Graphic Design
in Conservative Times

T0261897

A joyful noise:
A *wish list* for design in conservative times,
or, a desire to finally get out of these times*

Ramon Tejada

Introduction

Design in Conservative[1] times is an idea that forces me to think and position myself as a designer of color. Front and center. Design is not used to, and perhaps has even been averse to, someone like me speaking with authority[2]. Therefore, I am going to present some ideas and hopes, a *Wish List* of sorts, that emerges from this very perspective.

My position emanates directly from my confrontation with the notions of political conservatism that have surfaced and re-surfaced in the last few years. I live in the United States with its complicated and disgraceful racial history. And so living as a person of color in the USA still often puts one in uncomfortable, sometimes very difficult positions. Likewise, being a person of color in Design can be bewildering, frustrating, and infuriating (yes, *still* in 2020).

In our post-President Barack Obama era, the river of hate and racism present since the country's inception has found a new voice and vibrancy. Since the 2016 elections, the reality of structural racism, both in the political arena and swirling in more social contexts, is rearing its ugly head again, in new and vile ways. That dark day in 2016 was a reckoning that forced me to confront my relationship with many aspects of my everyday life, one of which was Design. I found an urgent need to start asking pointed questions. To use MY voice and begin to puncture through the sanitized veneer of Design, its Traditions and its preference for privilege, homogeneity, exclusivity, wealth and elitism. From my current perspective, many of these Traditions uphold the status quo, and in essence harken back to "the good old days." The irony is, of course, that they are often espoused and propagated by people that would be horrified to be called or be associated in any way, shape, or form as politically conservative. On the contrary, they probably see themselves as progressive.

Pushing against the current wave of cultural conservatism and an inherently slow-moving conservative culture of Art and Design, I have decided to rethink the values of my practice. I want my practice to be one that involves a more authentic engagement and that means having difficult conversations about Design, teaching Design, making Design and its relationship to

A joyful noise

human beings. Starting to push Design towards different spaces and perhaps towards redefining what it really could be.

I propose that we quickly dispense with Design, with a capital "D," and let a new wave of thinking and making take root that is a more genuine, authentic, and representative version of *designs*.

Rooted in the above, here are some ideas, questions and thoughts in the form of my *Wish List* for how we can go about achieving said new *designs*.

WISH LIST 1:
El Problema

Design (or what we catalogue and award privilege to as Design) is conservative. What we call Design is a 20th-century construct—codified from a Western European perspective. It embraces ideas of Tradition: hierarchy, authority, expertise, foundational skills, and universality.

.

Design is very singular.
What Design looks like, what is considered "good" Design, who makes "good" Design; who it privileges,
who and what it has elevated and legitimized is an exclusive and homogenous group. Its "foundation" excludes all but White, European Men. This is the vaunted and seemingly intractable *Grand Tradition* of our field.

.

Why do we cling so tightly to the past? Do we authentically examine the shameful colonial history of Europe and the United States? Isn't Design the progeny of this history?

.

Ramon Tejada

Striving for the quality, rigor, and values based on an established "good" is, in itself, conservative thinking. Even when we have "good" intentions, our intentions may be biased and compromised. We must acknowledge and *actively pivot from* this deep well of misogyny and racism that is the very foundation of Design.

•

Europe and the Bauhaus are not the Tigris and Euphrates of Design. It's *a* starting point for *a* particular type of Design that needs further contextualization and questioning and less worshiping and aggrandizing. For millennia, people from cultures *all* over the world have and continue to create artistic work yet much of this has been all but ignored in Art and Design.

•

Design apostles need to stop preaching inclusivity and diversity in dishonest, conservative ways, and then failing to reflect these homilies when the preaching is done and the work begins.

•

As a designer of color, and having been born in the Dominican Republic[3], this is about making and taking space. Some of us must simply take the space because it is clear that it will not be ceded. People that look like me must talk, write, make, explore our ideas and ways of seeing without the seeds of doubt planted by Disciples of the "Masters[4]." What I am speaking about is physical visibility, structural change, representation, not Tokenism, acknowledgements of ideas, land, values that were stolen, repressed, narratives, points of view, perspectives, stories, theories, ideas, geographical references, and a diversity of lineages. It is about unearthing, shifting the glance, decentering, giving agency, being vulnerable, making mistakes, ideation, thinking locally, and making the periphery a center[5].

A joyful noise

•

Conservatism is not wanting to give up the spotlight,
always fitting ideas into the existing boxes.
Always framing divergent ideas and perspectives
in relation to the status quo
(Western European and White as the de facto
starting point for all bases).

•

Knowledge and expertise are not only gained
by studying privileged information in singular places
(academies, elevated institutions).
Divergent learning and thinking are necessary for us
to remove this strand of conservatism in which we traffic.

•

History is skewed. If you don't believe me,
open up a Design history book (or most history books)
and see who is represented, how they are presented, and,
more importantly, who is not there.

•

We should be making *designs* that emanate from us
as human beings, not as heralds of Design.
If that leads us to making less stuff, then so be it.

•

Stop with singular, universal ideas.
Move away from the -uni and towards the *-multi*.
Design jealously guards the status quo.
This oh so colonial tendency needs to be called out,
and STOPPED, *ahora mismo*.

•

Ramon Tejada

Let's not make 21st-century *designs*
(and our world) a copy of 20th-century Design.
Absolutely NOT!

•

"Historically, pandemics have forced humans to break with
the past and imagine their world anew. This one is no
different. It is a portal, a gateway between one world and
the next. We can choose to walk through it, dragging
the carcasses of our prejudice and hatred, our avarice,
our data banks and dead ideas, our dead rivers and
smoky skies behind us.
Or we can walk through lightly, with little luggage, ready
to imagine another world. And ready to fight for it."
—Arundathi Roy, Financial Times, April 2020[6]

Aside: pandemic as opportunity*

I write these words in the midst of the Covid-19 global pandemic
(before the death of George Floyd at the hands of the Minneap-
olis police department which created an enormous wave of
pro-active social and political activism that is asking us all to
examine how White Supremacy and its tenets has created such
an unbalanced culture). A moment and time that is forcing us
ALL to communally shift, quickly and responsibly. We acknowledge the suffering, death and real darkness of this time.
We also optimistically question what good we can make from it?
This is an essential idea, right now and always.

WISH LIST 2:
STOP, ahora mismo

•

Stop talking *AT* and begin talking *with ahora mismo.*
Or take the time to press pause for a while on your own
speaking and instead actively listen.

•

Stop problem solving, ahora mismo.
We have created a lot more problems
with what we have made.
design does not need to solve problems,
it should present possibilities, and imaginative ideas.

•

Stop gatekeeping[7], ahora mismo.
Not just of people, but also their ideas,
perspectives, ways of seeing, stories and the validity
and legitimacy of that thinking.
Throw the gates wide open.

•

Stop saying you are not for maintaining the status quo,
yet you maintain it and uphold it every day
through relying on and aggrandizing the colonial
"Traditions" of Art and Design ahora mismo.

•

Stop making "innovative" Design that perpetuates
and elevates singular, elitist, universal,
and privileged ways, ahora mismo.

•

Ramon Tejada

•

Stop knowing everything.
Stop being an expert
or rather pretending to be ahora mismo.
"*Be humble, sit down*" to quote Kendrick Lamar[8].

•

WISH LIST 3:
"Walk through Lightly[9] or towards a new portal"

•

The future is here. Speculate for the now.
Let's stop patting ourselves on the back for aspiring,
start acting NOW!

•

No more homogeneity. We have had enough of it.
It has created too many problems, too much inequity,
and too much hierarchy: too much conservatism.

•

Realize the difference between healthy admiration and
canonization. Ideas are essential;[10] hero-worshipping
and the cult of personality is dangerous.

•

Think about how one enters a community
and engages in *respectful* dialogues.

•

A joyful noise

●

We must adopt models that are more open,
inclusive, collaborative, and we must consider all humans
as coming from a variety of places, experiences,
frames of reference, cultures, affordances, genders,
and divergent thinking.

●

Collaboration is an open, honest, and vulnerable structure.
Not the "collaborations" that are masking and
creating inequality, that lead to underappreciated,
undervalued, underpaid labor, shameful
and shameless appropriation.

●

*"In the rush to return to normal, let's use this time to
consider which parts of normal are worth rushing back to."*
—Dave Hollis

●

No more *White Space*. Literally and Conceptually.
The obvious and splendid irony of the double entendre
just cannot be left without comment.
The world is messy, crowded, bumpy[11], and beautiful;
it always has been. White space is dull, status quo,
not fluid, and conservative.

●

design for communities,
not just for luxury and exclusivity.
Be honest about what and for whom you are *designing*.[12]

●

Ramon Tejada

·

Reflect, and actively change your language,
and its damaging effects. It will continue to be if we don't
examine it and start to shift it or to position it
alongside alternatives.

·

EGOS NEED TO GET OUT OF THE WAY.
No one has time or space for your ego.

·

Think about who and what ideologies *you* are elevating
and giving space to?

·

Make for mom and dad.

·

WISH LIST 4:
Teaching as an antidote (interlude)

·

For those of us who teach *designs*:
teach as open collaborations. Teach using a
different model beyond the "master"
yikes there's that word again! student relationship.
Teaching should be open, about conversations
and possibilities, with vulnerability.
It should be truly experimental and messy.

·

A joyful noise

•

A BIG WISH:
Those of us that have been indoctrinated,
need to unlearn, and re-learn, so we don't teach
and perpetuate the same habits and structures.
Unlearning is hard as hell just as bell hooks writes.[13]

•

My teaching, which is a large part of my practice,
had to shift. It has put me in a place
where I am interested in re-learning, re-reading
and engaging with material that did not come across my eyes
in my education. Material usually created by incredibly
intelligent and creative people; a lot who look like me.
"Visibility = possibility[14]," as actress Constance Wu said.
Think of the value of seeing yourself reflected.
What that meant to you and what that means
to your students.

•

As a teacher, I think of myself as a sponge,
gelatinous in my approach: looser, messier and
more vulnerable when learning alongside my students.

•

Be vulnerable.
Real humans cry, laugh, and make mistakes.

•

Be fluid.
Covid-19 has shown us all how fluid we need to be.
How dexterous, creative and imaginative
we should be all the time.

•

Ramon Tejada

ʄIN:

I am optimistic about *designs* and the new things, artifacts, fields we are starting to create. They speak more inclusively and represent many more perspectives.

This moment (Covid-19 and the Death of George Floyd, Breonna Taylor and so many others in the USA and around the world) is demanding that we quickly come up with ways that do not blind us against continuing to make "sanitized stylistic choices that mask conservative normativity.[15]"

We must interrupt our repetitive systems — *design* systems, *design* language, ways of working in *design*. Who gets to work as a designer? Who is making *design?* — Repetition by nature shifts at a particular moment.

Right now is that moment! ¡Ahora mismo es el momento![16]

A joyful noise

1

A list of words and phrases encountered in the definitions of Conservatism and Design while perusing the Oxford English Dictionary: the tendency to resist change; adherence to traditional values and ideas; resist evolutionary change; a scheme; the preliminary conception of an idea that is to be carried into effect by action; scheme involving cunning or hypocrisy; the process, practice, or art of devising, planning, or constructing something according to aesthetic or functional criteria.

2

Some thoughts I wrote in 2018: "As a designer, I have come to terms with the fact that what and who design history has been interested in canonizing, up to this point, does not reflect me, my cultures, my values, and many of the tenets that make me a citizen, a designer, and a teacher. I don't see myself reflected in much of the narrative of design…"

3

Dominican Republic, or Hispaniola. An island nation in the Caribbean where the brutal criminal Christopher Columbus first landed and began the systematic rape, pillage and murder of millions. Which of these most closely shares its provenance with today's Design?. Columbus arrived at a land rich with history and people, who were brutalized and decimated by European settlement and exploitation. ¨La Española¨ was a land brimming with culture and ideas that were deemed unworthy, even diabolical by European settlers. For more of this art and design see, Arte del mar: Artistic exchanges in the Caribbean.

4

There is an insidious tradition in Design and certain artistic circles, for those in power to question the value, quality, and rigor (a questionable and potentially discriminatory term) of work made by people of color and women. This work has historically been seen as of less quality, less intellectual acuity, of less worth, and not as important to human development.

5

an ode to Toni Morrison's ideas about centrality and the gaze.

6

https://www.ft.com/content/10d8f5e8-74eb-11ea-95fe-fcd274e920ca

7

The urban dictionary's definition includes: When someone (or a field at large) takes it upon themselves to decide who has access to something. I would add, who has access and who is allowed and given the privilege to add and engage within a field. In the context of Art and Design, homogeneity in our fields has created many problems concerning whose stories and perspectives get acknowledgment and respect. See The Gatekeepers: Expanding America's Cultura Power Structure, https://www.aspeninstitute.org/videos/gatekeepers-expanding-americas-cultural-power-structure/

8

https://www.youtube.com/watch?v=tvTRZJ-4EyI

9

The Pandemic is a Portal, Arundathi Roy, Financial Times. https://www.ft.com/content/10d8f5e8-74eb-11ea-95fe-fcd274e920ca

10

Let's teach a history of ideas, not the history of individuals, Juliette Cezzar, AIGA Eye on Design. https://eyeondesign.aiga.org/lets-teach-a-history-of-ideas-not-the-history-of-individuals/

11

The idea of Bumpiness is attributed to Prem Krishnamurthy in his experimental publication P!DF.

12

I say this with the utmost respect. Understanding that people come from all sorts of cultural, social, and financial circumstances and that at times we all have to

Ramon Tejada

earn a living and sustain ourselves. We
need to be careful that we do not use this
as an exclusionary tactic.

13
Teaching to Transgress, bell hooks.

14
Wu commented about this during
the press junkets for the film Crazy
Rich Asians in 2018. For more
see https://time.com/5355015/
constance-wu-crazy-rich-asians-tweet/

15
Allan de Souza, How Art Can Be Thought,
page 158.

16
We have been speculating and fantasizing
about the future too much. Here it is.
Perhaps it has been here all along.

Additional sources and notes:

* notes on being a DOMINICANYORK...,
  Ramon Tejada, various formats, tests,
  experiments of a work in progress.
  An attempt at puncturing and inserting
  the Dominican into design.
* Chimamanda Ngozi Adichie,
  The Danger of a Single Story
* Toni Morrison's work, novels, essays,
  everything.
* bell hooks, Teaching to Transgress,
  Teaching Community, among others.
* John Leguizamo, Latin History
  for Morons
* Josefina Baez, Dominicanish
* James Baldwin read it all.
* Collaborating and "Throwing The
  Bauhaus Under The Bus," with Silas
  Munro at Otis College Of Art And Design
  in Los Angeles, summer, 2019.
* W.E.B. Du Bois's Data Portraits
* Allan deSouza, How Art Can Be Thought
* Octavia Butler's writings.

Additional readings:

Design Thinking is a Rebrand for White
Supremacy, Darin Buzon, Medium
https://medium.com/@dabuzon/
design-thinking-is-a-rebrand-for-white-
supremacy-b3d31aa55831

Graphic Design's Factory Setting,
Jacob Lindgren
https://walkerart.org/magazine/
jacob-lindgren-graphic-designs-factory-
settings

Making and Being, Susan Jahoda and
Caroline Woolard
https://makingandbeing.com/

What does decolonizing design Mean,
Anoushka Khandwala
https://eyeondesign.aiga.org/
what-does-it-mean-to-decolonize-design/
Who's Bad? Jerome Harris
https://2019.typographics.com/schedule/
jerome-harris/

W.E.B. Du Bois's Data Portraits:
Visualizing Black America, Silas Munro
https://letterformarchive.org/
events/w.e.b.-du-boiss-data-portraits-
visualizing-black-america

Ruined by design, how designers
destroyed the world, and what they can do
to fix it, Mike Monteiro
https://www.ruinedby.design

This bridge called my back, Writings by
radical women of color, edited by Cerrie
Moraga, Gloria Anzaldua
https://www.amazon.com/This-Bridge-
Called-Back-Fourth/dp/1438454384/
ref=sr_1_1?dchild=1&keywords=This
+bridge+called+my+back&qid=15872
47962&sr=8-1

Urgentcraft, Paul Soulellis
https://soulellis.com/writing/urgentcraft2/

The Black Experience in Graphic Design:
1968 and 2020
https://letterformarchive.org/news/
the-black-experience-in-graphic-
design-1968-and-2020
https://www.printmag.com/post/
the-black-experience-1968

Sadie Red Wing // F* The Stereotype:
Revitalizing Indigenous Perspective in
Design
https://www.youtube.com/watch?v=
HVZtem89VFQ&fbclid=IwAR0G_
U1qby6HKz1K8YE UF5P4O1nrlX2A2Ljj
1Gqbvx8jw5YPh1K6kPB9BKU

Decentering whiteness in design history:
Resources
https://docs.google.com/document/d
/1KiW2ULDFelm_OuvwhM2lygxwhoNddr
EFk5tYI9zbldw/edit

fig. 1

　A joyful noise

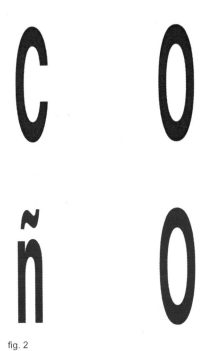
fig. 2

19   Ramon Tejada

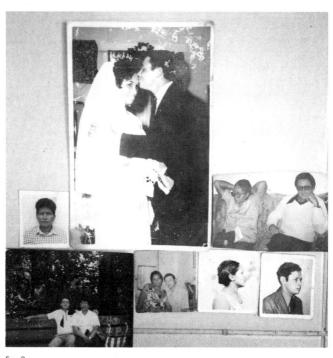

fig. 3

A joyful noise

fig. 1–3   courtesy of the author

Ramon Tejada

Typography in Conservative Times

Huda Smitshuijzen-AbiFarès

Typography has become an intrinsic part of modern print and new media, and its communicative power has grown exponentially in contemporary societies of the third millennium. Type and letterforms are the smallest and most basic blocks of visual communication. These small abstract forms are carriers of meanings, messages, and at times, vital information. The way they are designed also carries clues to long standing traditions and cultural histories. The way the design of certain letterforms expresses the subtleties and functionalities of the act of reading in specific cultures has become a growing concern in the type design world. This concern often triggers passionate discussions and creates demarcation lines between opposing and rigid political standpoints. The confrontation of these opposing viewpoints marks a surprising development at a time when technological possibilities have paved the way for an extensive range of ideologically driven or aesthetically driven design explorations. A time when what can be researched and produced has become practically limitless. One therefore wonders why conservative approaches still prevail, and why those that stray from the 'right path' are often publicly vilified or ridiculed.

Multiscript families and the politics of harmonizing disparate cultures

In the context of the recent health epidemic that has in turn capitulated us into a worldwide economic recession, our inevitable connectedness has shown us that our global interdependence, if not acknowledged and respected, can lead to disastrous outcomes. We are connected, we have shared responsibilities towards our planet, we need each other to thrive and survive, and so we should respect each other and agree on common rules and ethics. One possible alternative is to scale things down so as to return to operating on a local or regional scale; a return to local traditional crafts and culture-specific design aesthetics is then a logical reaction, that may lead to interesting new developments. This is indeed a time of reflection on how design can serve society and engage with political and social emergencies.

In the world of typeface design, this means an interest in hand-written letterforms, a return to hand-cut metal or wood type, searching for the human hand and the tactile quality, and bridging traditional methods of designing contemporary digital fonts. Another aspect of type design that is ideologically motivated is the creation of more culturally meaningful projects. This has taken the direction of upholding scripts that have not been adequately designed for modern media as a means of preserving cultural diversity. It is important to support diversity in the face of a diluting and equalizing manner of globalization, where one culture (and its script) dominates all. Yet is it equally important to look at history from different perspectives to learn how writing systems are connected, and how they have developed and influenced each other over the centuries—a process facilitated by human networks of commerce and exchange, along the silk routes of olden times and the various trading posts and cities of ancient empires.

Typography's inherent ability to give knowledge a 'fixed shape', and disseminate it across wide geographic regions, has brought several cultures together. It has made diverse scripts sit side-by-side; forcing them to converse and find common ground. Contemporary international commerce has further contributed to the creation of truly multicultural and multilingual urban societies across the world. The fluidity of interaction and exchange between people of different cultures has increased the need for multilingual (and multiscript) graphic design. Modern media and technological advancements have bridged design and aesthetic considerations across cultural and geographical borders. Designers are challenged today to respond to the needs of contemporary communications[1] and to harmoniously bring various writing systems together under one unifying, visual system in order to reduce visual dissonance and noise. Fortunately, there are countless design approaches and solutions to address
this visual complexity.

There is no denying that the Latin script, which accommodates the languages of Europe and the Americas—or, in other words, the languages of international trade and business—is often paired with the national languages (or scripts) of

25   Huda Smitshuijzen-AbiFarès

practically all nations around the globe. Multiscriptual designs are applied to wayfinding systems, public spaces, transport terminals (airports, train stations, subway systems), advertising billboards, posters, branding, packaging, corporate literature, books, publications, apps, websites, and products of all kinds. The dominance of the Latin script is felt more acutely in type design practices to a point where the world of typefaces is divided into two main categories: Latin and (all the other) 'Non-Latin' scripts. The sheer number of fonts and typefaces created for the Latin script may be one reason for this imbalance, however the more likely reason is the typesetting and printing equipment—from the printing press to digital font-authoring tools. This equipment was originally invented and marketed worldwide by countries where the Latin script is native, and so were better suited for Latin typography. Indic, Asian and Arabic scripts, for example, are fundamentally different from Latin in their structure, alignment, construction and historical evolution. In addition, writing systems each have their own conventions for legibility and aesthetic consideration. Not all world scripts fit within a bounding box or align on a horizontal baseline. In recent years, several technological and cultural attempts have been made to rectify this disparity.

And so the political is inevitably scripted in the design of typefaces, especially for 'Non-Latin' writing systems. Looking for common ground between scripts—especially when we combine the 'dominant Latin' with the less widely-used or 'Non-Latin' script—often involves sensitivities that go beyond purely practical considerations. Most designers struggle with creating harmony while still preserving the respective integrity of the scripts through their design. The easiest option is to return to existing historical models at the expense of creating font families that are not quite visually compatible but that may be congruent in a historical sense. When designers are more inclined to be experimental, or to try and explore new or unusual styles for Non-Latin scripts, they are often criticised and accused of 'Latinizing' those scripts. This implies that experimentation is only the prerogative of Latin type; other scripts have to stick to the exoticising Western perception of what they should look like. Recent years have seen several initiatives explore creating a type design that is not an adaptation of another script or an

Typography in Conservative Times

existing script but is a collaboration between different native designers that together create a multiscript font family that is a cross-pollination between different aesthetic and cultural characteristics.

Multiscript typeface design and cultural considerations

In recent years, the mixing of serif and sans serif typefaces within one font family has become widely used to the point that it is often expected by end-users and clients. As a result of biscriptual typesetting and harmonizing with the Latin script, Non-Latin scripts have developed equivalent classifications: high-contrast to match serif typefaces (for long reading texts), and low-contrast to match sans serif typefaces (for small and display type sizes)—a politically motivated nomenclature that avoids imposing the foreign 'Latin' conventions on these scripts. Another design trend across scripts is to create an extensive set of weights for the same typeface design. The old scribal conventions of mixing script styles to demarcate hierarchies within a text have been replaced by more subtle solutions of mixing stroke contrast, weights, and type sizes.

The proportions and visual rhythms of different scripts are one of the major challenges for designing multiscript typefaces and achieving visual compatibility when typesetting different scripts at the same visual size. Matching the proportions of various scripts can be done roughly by looking at the overall concentration of density in their letterforms. For example, Latin typefaces with large x-heights (or small caps) match best with monocase and mono-width scripts like Chinese, Hangul and Hebrew. Whereas Latin typefaces with old-style proportions and small x-heights (as well as long ascenders and descenders) match better Arabic text faces. In text blocks, some scripts require more leading than others. Looking for similar details within the drawing of the letterforms (the way the strokes are constructed, the proportions of counters, the stroke thicknesses, the fluidity or geometry of the letterforms) can contribute to a subtle visual connection and harmony amongst the various scripts.

Huda Smitshuijzen-AbiFarès

A typeface defines the visual identity of a design and has a particular 'tone of voice' that is often governed by the way it has been used historically. The connotations of certain type styles are culture-specific and have been developed over centuries of conventions, adding an extra parameter for matching scripts within one design. Deciding on a typeface is commonly dictated by the design function; there are typefaces that have been used traditionally for specific media (ie. newspapers, literary publications, signage…etc), therefore, the choice of font for each script should be mindful of these conventions. A designer may decide to exploit the familiarity of the reader with these conventions, or intentionally diverge from these traditional choices to make a particular statement. An attempt to bring a similar tone of voice for a translated text, means the text block needs to become a 'visual translation' into another language—particularly when these scripts have to be set side by side. Combining similar looking typefaces gives an overall sense of order and reduces visual noise. However, there are times when the contrast between two languages needs to be exaggerated in order to visually differentiate the languages and thus help with the act of reading the text—especially when the languages use the same or similar scripts (ie. Latin, Greek and Cyrillic).

Typography as a political tool

A script or writing system remains the first visual representative of a particular culture, religion or community. Conservative approaches prevail as cultures are in the process of finding equal footing on a Western-dominated world stage. As technical constraints diminish, formal design experimentations flourish. This has so far led to a dramatic rise in the design and creation of new typefaces. Nonetheless, the challenge of balancing technical, aesthetic, cultural, and practical limitations persists and still requires the inventiveness of designers and their conscious engagement in intelligently countering conservative or overly politicized views. The choices often made by designers go beyond the practical and aesthetic constraints; their choices impact the cultures for which they are designing. Therefore, type and graphic designers should be conscious of the implications of their choices and employ their skills to honourable ends.

Today, and more than ever before, there is a need to use typography in supporting cultural diversity, and in challenging conventional attitudes in search for innovation that upholds marginalised cultures and minorities. Designers must assume the responsibilities that come with their act of creation; what they create today will have a lasting impact on future generations and will shape how we live and interact with the world surrounding us. To design is to be ethically and politically engaged; and typography can be a powerful political tool to this end.

1
Communications meaning the various systems used for sending especially electronic information, such as radio, television, telephone, and computer networks.

29   Huda Smitshuijzen-AbiFarès

fig. 1

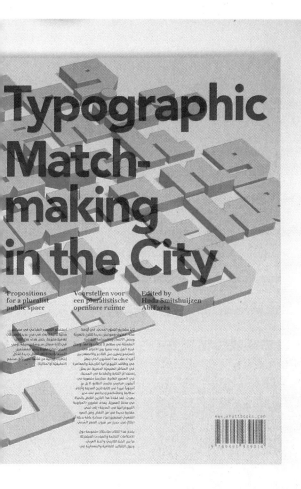

31 Huda Smitshuijzen-AbiFarès

fig. 2

32   Typography in Conservative Times

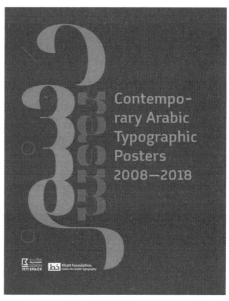

fig. 3

fig. 1–3 · courtesy of the author

Huda Smitshuijzen-AbiFarès

Design for disarming times

Annelys de Vet

In this text, the perspective of conservatism is drawn to something of 'inherent' value, and explores notions of cultural heritage, indigenous knowledges and the current political conditions they exist within. All through the perspective of design. This interest arose from my experience of setting up create shops in Palestine for the design platform 'Disarming Design from Palestine'. During our yearly workshops, local and international designers worked with Palestinian craft practices and developed useful objects that underscored connections between tradition, innovation and the political narratives they exist within. By deeply engaging with the field of crafts and design in Palestine, I witnessed what colonial occupation is, and what it can do to people, identity and land. Urging us to question the role of design in the processes of emancipation and expression of marginalized identities.

How can design help counteract unjust realities and contribute to social transformation? Listening to the stories of artisans and designers profoundly changed me as a global (and local) citizen and as an engaged practitioner. It taught me about life through the medium of craft, materiality, resources, land, collaboration, solidarity, as well as the political implications they each can have. This is a story about what can be learned from designers and artisans in Palestine. How can we use processes of design as a tool to learn from our worlds?

Craftsmanship & Materiality

Last summer, with the create shop, we visited a wood workshop near Ramallah in the occupied West bank, where the carpenter proudly showed us examples of the complicated and admirable woodwork he used to make for his clients. He explained that customers hardly ask for this skilled work of his anymore as they either find it too expensive or fail to understand the urgency of it – neither do they see the quality. And so, the demand for this competent labour is reducing, with orders becoming less specific, questions more generic, making it harder (and less joyful) for artisans to compete with machines and mass production. The artisan explained how economically fragile his position was and admitted he didn't know how long he would be able to

Design for disarming times

keep his workshop open in this manner. Leading him to question how much longer his specific knowledge will be kept alive; a knowledge that is passed down through different generations, and entangled in social structures. Are there new generations that will follow on? If his clients could better understand the relationship between local productions and the knowledge and social structures it empowers, would that change their orders?

These are the indigenous knowledges embodied by craftsmanship, and not something that can be learnt from a book or a YouTube video. It is the knowledge of generations that goes through the body and is best transmitted in the workshop itself; with the materials, tools, their possibilities and limitations, and with human encounters. In the Netherlands (where I grew up) and in Belgium (where I live) I hardly see artisans at work in cities — those at work often serve a more exclusive market. Workshops for wood, metal and leather for instance, are mostly upscaled or have been moved to more industrial areas, or the production is outsourced to low-income-countries. Our dependence on the global market of production has become even more clear during the corona crisis, which fueled a call for local small-scale production. While in the center of cities such as Ramallah, Nablus and Jerusalem one can still (although notably less and less) find several small workshops as part of everyday life; molding metal, making shoes or glazing pottery. To me, this was eye opening; to be aware of these production processes and experience them while passing by or entering the shops introduced me to a rich cultural heritage and made me better understand the social structures that surrounded them, how families are connected, how complicated it can be to transport resources or machines in and products out of the country, how so many artisans have faced military raids in their workspaces and more harsh realities. Alongside this it taught me the effects of colonial occupation and how it oppresses every part of daily life, movement, material, law, economy; everything. This was a fundamental experience. To learn about the occupation through materiality allowed me to deeply see the impact of the disrupted socio-political situation.

To many, the Israel-Palestine 'conflict' emerged mainly from religious or nationalistic issues, while the reality is different because "the occupation is much more related to economic

Annelys de Vet

motives within a capitalist 'game'", as is explained by Palestinian permaculture designer Mohammad Saleh. The Israeli economy is directly fed by military technology and security systems, and the private sector plays an explicit role in the Israeli settlement enterprise and in the economic exploitation of Palestinian and Syrian land, labour and resources.[1] As an act of resistance Mohammad Saleh believes it is important to focus on the production of local designs, especially as a way of acting rather than reacting. "With more local production models, we practice crucial steps of self-sovereignty. It will help artisans to sustain their businesses, families and inherited craftsmanship. This empowers a local economy. The design comes from within and relates to local needs and points of view. This is a socially conscious action, rather than a re-action to the behaviours of others"

With the create shops that Disarming Design from Palestine organizes, we start the design processes with visiting workshops, meeting artisans and listening to their stories, seeing them at work and trying to understand their mechanisms. Most of their knowledge is picked up in practice, in daily life, and not through formal education. As Palestinian designer Qusai Saify explains: „What we learned through working with artisans is to be awake all the time and to be sensitive to each detail you are working on, either how you behave or how you are going to develop the design itself. We live in our heads when we think of a design, but when you really work with the artisans you discover lots of layers. As a designer one can pay attention to the details the artisans are living in and from that you get your feedback to the design itself. If you are aware of this feedback you will learn a lot, if you want to ignore that feedback, or if you are not that sensitive maybe you learn a lot less. Each time something is not working, you need to deal with the situation in a creative way. And with this kind of creativity you don't have the answer yourself, but you have to find answers together to develop ideas with the artisan. This is a moment when you are reshaping yourself; I felt I was redesigning myself through the designs I was working on."

Design is a practice of thought and often holds you in a hypothetical individual space behind the computer. When you are working digitally your body often stays more or less in the same position, but when you are making things together your

Design for disarming times

physical movements become part of the energy of the process. Meeting the artisan brings a complete other dimension. Bodies start to interact, you relate to one another, look one another in the eyes, see one's hands, and feel the materials. This is a relational design process where the body acts in the design development and becomes an important instrument; a tool to make. There is a physical counterforce of the materials and a social interaction between people with very different skill-sets who normally wouldn't interact. Often there is a class difference between artisans with lived knowledge and designers from a more formally educated background. They have economic differences, sometimes cultural or racial differences and possibly a language barrier. Visiting the artisan in their working environment places them in the position of strength of knowledge; it puts the skill of crafts and making central to the conversation and allows a mutual space to develop ideas. There is an almost magical exchange taking place in the encounters of testing and making things together; an access to a deeper knowledge, materialized in the acts of making. In doing so, it feels that the moment we better understand how things are made, we achieve a more humane material existence. Making together influences relationships between people and gives space to mediate initial inequalities, therefore allowing for an emancipatory potential. These are precognitive processes that go beyond language, beyond a reflective attitude and offer participation in different ways.

Often in design education the focus is more on aspects of the conceptual, aesthetic or technical, rather than on the role of the body, the sensorial and the design processes that come with it. While this is an important element, even more so when we talk about participative practices and when working with people from different backgrounds. Bodies matter and influence a sense of trust, connectivity and creativity. It's something we should take into account, question and sensitize while working together in the same space.

Land & Resources

Some of my most impactful experiences in Palestine were the hikes I made over the green and yellow hills that boasted

Annelys de Vet

century old olive trees, empty riverbeds, rocky landscapes with a vibratory panorama, or walks far below sea level near the Dead Sea. Hiking alone in the West bank is not recommended due to the unpredictable danger of the military occupation. Therefore I joined different groups of people who hike on a weekly basis, to escape the daily tensions and find protection in being together. Each time I walked the landscape it left a deep impression and I was overwhelmed by its scale and history, as well as being witness to the loss of land, the brutal destruction and the theft of water. Along the way I exchanged thoughts with people I had never met before about absolutely anything that had triggered us from what we saw, tasted or smelled. These conversations helped me to relate to the place I was in and to understand the deeply lived relation the people have with it. Many family stories were shared about picking wild herbs, especially 'za'tar', the Palestinian thyme, but also sage and mint – or whatever we could find around to make fresh tea for the shared picknick. I was introduced to new tastes with the carob bean, that looks like dark brow dried pea pod, but has an almost fresh liquorish kind of taste (delicious, especially while hiking). I was bewildered about the sometimes centuries old olive trees that were taken care of continuously, from generation to generation. And I admired the innumerable terraces dotted everywhere around on the hills that looked like geological layers, and realised that each single terrace is human made, over centuries of moving stones, making the soil fertile. But also the barbarous scale of the illegal settlements was visible, as well as the mortal pace with which the water level of the dead sea is falling and I was left in disbelief when my interlocutors were telling me about the new Israeli law that forbids Palestinians to pick wild herbs and plants.

The energy of being outside and walking together is an important condition for relating to each other, and our direct environment. Mohammad Saleh places this partly in the healing capacity of nature: „when negativity started taking over me, I looked inside myself and asked: what am I passionate about? And the answer was nature. And this was the starting point for acting upon my own choices: I created gardens, green spots in the places where I lived. You could think that this is not related to politics, society and psychology, but it is. When a person

Design for disarming times

finds a green nice spot, this heals him, and in Palestine we are all wounded, so we are all in need of healing. In doing so, I am not reacting to the negative circumstances, which are dictated by others, but still have a crucial impact on them." What does nature do and how to start as a designer from that perspective? For Qusai Saify social rituals like harvesting, olive picking and hiking are meaningful for new ideas and fundamental insights. He wants to design in a way that supports a basic lifestyle. In the context of Palestine, with its limited access to resources and disrupted import, it is utterly relevant to question how to design with limited as well as local materials.

In a reality where land is so disputed, where grounds are stolen and where history is violently erased, the relation to the place is of existential importance. The land provides existence, identification, and allows one to take root in a place. It can contribute to both healing and self-sovereignty. Therefore, the role of nature, the relation to a place and the understanding of natural cycles is an indispensable aspect in decolonial design learning.

Storytelling & Identity

How can you speak outside of the questions that are imposed on you, how to make the truth about colonial occupation visible, how to show the human aspect of life in Palestine and how to give just enough information that it doesn't become exploitable in any structure of oppression? During the symposium 'Out of Sight' at the Qattan Foundation in Ramallah in the autumn of 2018, Palestinian filmmaker Kamal Jafari mentioned how several of his friends say that their families hardly ever explained to them what had happened to other family members during the Nakba in 1948.[2] Like his friends, Kamal asked his grandmother several times about what happened to her back then. She was never able to tell him. But then, when she was very old, Kamal decided to film her. This turned out to be the first time that she was able to speak to him: in 1948 she escaped by boat from Haifa towards Lebanon, but there was a big storm so her boat went back to the shore. That is how she survived within the 1948 borders, and not, for instance, end up in a refugee camp in Lebanon. For Kamal this was an important story to contex-

Annelys de Vet

tualize his own identity. He stressed how important it is as a filmmaker to share and express how people experience something, and what such a situation means on a human level.

Storytelling can be seen as a form of resilience and resistance, because it also allows space for the expression of identity, which is both problematic and vital if these identities are marginalized. Interior designer Ghadeer Dajani says that the stories don't need to always be about Palestine, "because sometimes we become prisoners in this circle of expectation that if you are a Palestinian then all your work has to be about Palestine. This can be too much, too intensive. Sometimes you need to detach yourself from the political situation, from occupation, from colonization, and design something just for the sake of designing." Areej Ashab mentions how she experienced this as a Palestinian student in an Israeli institution in Jerusalem: "Sometimes we are seen more as Palestinians than as design students and we are pushed to deal with issues related to the political situation and how it affects our lives. As we become subjects of exoticism, sometimes it is more interesting for them [Israeli teachers] to hear us talking about what we go through rather than listening to what Israelis do. This perception puts us in uncomfortable situations having to always confront and expose the conflicted reality we live in. They see it from a very orientalist point of view, and through our reflection in their eyes we fear we also adopt this point of view. This issue is very sensitive and it's important to think about it in relation to design education; how can we remove ourselves from this identity and try to be just designers, just ourselves?"

During her participation in the interdisciplinary create shops, together with foreign participants Areej valued the exchange. "It was interesting to see how international designers translated the reality they see here, compared to those of us who had always lived here and who often take for granted how we live. Together this resulted in interesting products and life-changing experiences." For instance, when the participants of the create shop passed the checkpoint in Qalandia, the international students were deeply shocked about the system, the way people are treated like animals and the inhumane confrontation with security. Together with Areej, they kept on talking about this experience and it led to the design of the 'Checkpoint

Design for disarming times

bag'; a leather backpack to support passing the checkpoint, and in doing so expressing part of the lived experience, by adding special details and a hidden message that is only visible under the x-ray; a silhouette of some old keys as a symbol for the right to return for refugees.

Although many of the cultural exchanges in our create shops have been considered positive, there have also been problematic moments. In some occasions the question of 'the outsider' was perceived as violent or disruptive to the safe atmosphere of the shared space. It can be a burden to teach others and to detail your own oppression, or experience of racism. One's stories can become just a recording for others who are not part of your reality, especially in a context in which "the westerner" is always the privileged party. Therefore, we talked a lot about how we can secure an equal space for learning and commitment with a group of people with very different lived realities, traumas, privileges and education. How we transfer a real understanding of a situation; how you can help in imagining it, feeling it, emerging through it. And how design can tell stories, fundamental stories of what it means to be in an oppressed position and how a political situation affects people's lives.

Solidarity & Resistance

Palestine has a very different context to Europe; geographically, politically, economically, historically and colonially. It is a reality where systems of oppression, exclusion and violence play distinct roles. Settler colonialism has resulted in the cultural, social, and physical displacement of indigenous peoples. In order to rationalize this violence, settler colonialism relies on narratives of hierarchical power that inevitably positions the settler state and its stakeholders at the top. It is a complicated and often difficult geo-political situation that makes Palestine a unique case; it is colonialism, but it is also not. It is post colonialism, but it is also not. From the outside it's hard to understand what it means to grow up on the inside. But if one begins to understand the colonial and military situation in Palestine, then many other patterns of oppression, class, and colonial or postcolonial structures become tragically visible. This allows for a deeper understanding that can inform a more conscious design practice dislodging dominant and oppressive colonial narratives, one that can imagine and also enact the world differently.

The experiences and encounters in Palestine have changed me, as a person and profoundly as a designer. It made me realize how my aims for quality were rooted in a modernist ideology and were far from inclusive. By working so closely with designers and artisans in Palestine, beyond the aesthetic and conceptual facets, I learned to value the relational and participatory potential of design, and how meaning and narratives are shaped through contexts and connections. Things are their relations; nothing exists by itself; everything is interconnected.

It often confronted me with my own privileged, and sometimes ignorant, position as a white European in a racially and violently occupied reality. When I visit Palestine with a group of "Western" designers, it is important to think of how to avoid reproducing colonial structures, instrumentalization or disruptive power relations. I became aware of pedagogical tools for engaged design practices where students come to realize their social and political position and the power structures they function within, giving space to other knowledges through a design process. It allowed us to move beyond existing definitions of both design and the political, and focus on stimulating international collaborations of solidarity. However, simply learning about colonial power relations does not in itself necessarily disrupt the dominant frames of knowing and being that are themselves made through those warped relations.

Design has the potential to respectfully relate to, and innovate local traditions of production, so as to value them within our current times and within their political dimensions. Thinking through design, rather than through words, allows the language and structure of design to engage different people and histories. It favours methods of working bottom-up within situated design methods and enables design as a praxis of world making. If we talk about conservatism as the conserving of traditional values, it is specifically this aspect that I want to put forward, and for which I call on designers to think critically about in their own practices. To better understand which systems they are

Design for disarming times

serving with their work. If we all do so, we might counteract the conservative neo-liberal systems that dominate the markets and that feed into subsequent systems of exploitation and suppression.

1
https://whoprofits.org

2
The 1948 Palestinian exodus, also known as the Nakba (Arabic: النكبة, al-Nakbah, literally "disaster", "catastrophe", or "cataclysm"), occurred when more than 700,000 Palestinian Arabs — about half of prewar Palestine's Arab population — forceful fled or were expelled from their homes, during the 1948 Palestine war. Between 400 and 600 Palestinian villages were sacked during the war, while urban Palestine was almost entirely extinguished The term nakba also refers to the period of war itself and events affecting Palestinians from December 1947 to January 1949.

Acknowledgments to Areej Ashab, Ghadeer Dajani, Pascal Gielen, Yazan Khalili, Rudy Luijters, Mohammed Saleh and Petra Vanbrabandt for their generous and inspirational input. This article is part of the PhD research 'Disarming Design from Palestine', supported by ARIA, a practice-led doctoral study at Sint Lucas School of Arts and University, Antwerp.

Annelys de Vet

fig. 1

Design for disarming times

fig. 2

fig. 3

Design for disarming times

fig. 1
Designer Ayat Bader (PS) at Jaba Glass
Factory (PS).
Photography: Florian Mecklenburg

fig. 2
Worksdiscussion during create shop in
Jerusalem, 2015
Photography: Mohammad Saleh

fig. 3
Hiking in Battir (near Bethlehem).
Photography: Teresa Palmieri

Annelys de Vet

Fashion Design
in Conservative Times

T0261907

Good Materialism –
A Proposal for
Conservationism in
Fashion

Marjanne Van Helvert

To dress extravagantly in war time is worse than bad form; it is unpatriotic

Quoted above is a particularly moralistic British motivational poster from the First World War. It was produced by the National War Savings Committee in 1916 as part of a domestic propaganda campaign to gain the general public's approval on the war effort. Statements such as those presented in the poster attempted to shame members of the public who appeared to not be carrying their weight in supporting the war, such as by wasting precious resources on whimsical things as fashion. War meant scarcity in nearly all fields of production and trade. There were not only shortages in the supply of food, but also in most consumer goods, including textiles. Local textile manufacturing was put into service for the war effort, notably for the production of soldier uniforms, meaning there was an immediate scarcity in the field of civilian clothes. While most people living a century ago were rarely presented with the opportunity to wear fancy, new clothes, those who could keep up appearances were urged to keep their fashions subdued. Sober attire was considered good taste in times of war; it meant that one was thrifty and careful not to waste their precious materials, energy, or labour, especially if they could otherwise be of use to the war industry.

Although I hesitate to find encouragement in such war propaganda, let alone calls for patriotism, I want to explore the concepts of moderation and conservation, rather than *conservatism*, in fashion. Particularly as we live in a time where we are rather brutally confronted with the limits to our fantasies of endless growth, and therefore may find inspiration from other times of crisis. Learning from times of material scarcity about the prevention of unnecessary waste.

Utility

Another war, another bout of propaganda. The Second World War saw many governments anticipating scarcity issues and installing various types of 'war socialism' to counter them.[1] In the UK particularly, extensive measures were taken to ensure

the public's material well-being. Well-known examples of war socialism are of course food rationing (with food stamps) and the national healthcare system, however lesser known is the Utility program. Despite there being a conservative government in the UK during the war, the state took control of the design, manufacture, distribution, marketing, and retail of many common consumer products, including clothing, furniture, and civilian goods, much in the same manner we associate with communist planning. The resulting system was referred to as the Utility scheme. Complete chains of production and consumption of consumer goods were reinvented and regulated in a somewhat successful attempt to provide people with what they needed as efficiently as possible. This meant not only designing durable goods with as little frills as possible, so as not to waste any precious material, labour, or energy, but it also meant mindful infrastructure and distribution systems for all products. This included preventing unnecessary transport, and therefore preserving time, energy and fuel. The result was a calculated network of local production facilities and retailers across the country, whilst at the same time becoming a prime example of the redistribution of wealth across all levels and classes of citizens.[2]

Make do and mend

Although not every country took these extensive socialist and centralized measures to counter scarcity issues during wartime, most were aware of the danger of shortages, and the negative effect this could have on public morale. As the availability of merchandise decreased, and shops emptied or closed, people were forced to "make do" with what they had, repair what they could, and recycle when possible. Governments across the world published campaigns to encourage people to be thrifty and creative with what they had, and instructions were issued on how to mend textiles and kitchen wares; how to repair and construct common items at home; how to save fuel, grow vegetables, and how to save your woollies from getting eaten by moths. Popular media including fashion magazines chimed

in with tips and tricks on DIY accessories and upcycling patterns avant la lettre. Ironically, many of these tips and instructions find their counterparts in the countless tutorials available on the internet today, urging us to upcycle our mountains of waste rather than the few precious materials we cherish until they fall apart. Leading to the question, is it time to look back instead of forward?

Not conservatism, not consumerism, but something else

I've always been intuitively opposed to any conservative move- ment. Conservatism means keeping things the way they are. It generally makes me think of old white guys desperately cling- ing to their crumbling empires of privilege and domination in the face of smarter, younger, more egalitarian ideas of solidarity. How could anyone want conservatism when there is progress to be made? *Equal rights for everyone! More women in charge! Abolish poverty!* Screw any tradition or taboo that conflicts with expressing your identity. Out with the old, in with the new!

Yet halfway through the 20th century, amidst a polit- ical landscape of transformation and civil rights, calls for revolu- tion and social change that have since dominated the popular memory of the western world became successfully exposed to an all-encompassing consumerism. The market gobbled up counterculture and spat out shopping malls. Youth culture be- came a big business; subcultures could hardly develop before being taken hostage by one brand or another. Individual freedom was found not so much in our minds or even in society, but instead in our wallets. Any freedom of choice became the choice of the consumer, any identity an assemblage of our shopping preferences: the styles we wear, the brands we use, the cars we drive all now determine who we are. We may still not be able to choose a female President (in the U.S.) or Prime Minister (in the Netherlands), but we can home order any product 24 hours a day. We cannot make the change to ditch fossil fuels, but we can pick any part of the globe as our next holiday destination. We can choose our styles and our looks, we can select any-

Good Materialism

thing in any color (no more "so long as it's black" as Henry Ford had once declared), and we can pick all kinds of alternatives to the mainstream, to set us apart just a little bit. In the immortal words of Mark Renton in the movie *Trainspotting*: "choose a fucking big television, choose washing machines, cars, compact disc players [this is the early 90s after all] and electrical tin openers... Choose life!". To which he added: "I chose not to choose life; I chose something else."

Wealth versus Welfare

Do we have to reach for the cynicism of Renton and his friends to move past the types of progress that capitalist society has served for us? Are we that far beyond that very idea of *progress*? Not the limitless pursuit of ever more material wealth, not quantity but quality: the increasing overall welfare and well-being for everyone. Progress is emancipation: it is social equality, environmental care, political freedom, ethical conscience. It is emancipation of all non-white, non-male, non-hetero, non-cis, non-western, non-colonial, non-able-bodied, non-upper and middle class, etc. people of this world, which together, by the way, form an overwhelming majority that should construct a strength of solidarity with each other. Progress is found in the well-being of all creatures on our planet, and of our planetary system that sustains us all. Out with the conservative traditions of hierarchy and colonialism, sexism, racism, classism, ableism, ageism, and all intersectional oppressions. Out with speciesism, in with the freedom of all creatures on this earth! Yet instead, we have kept to old economic systems and social orders, and we have been reduced to channeling our longing for progress into an endless succession of more, better, and slightly different commodities. Out with the old iPhone, in with the new!

Good News

The good news is that this type of mass consumerism is a relatively new phenomenon. In its current gigantic scale, it is hardly a century old (counting from the introduction of planned obso-

lescence in the design and manufacture of consumer products at the time of the financial crisis of the 1930s.) This time frame spans around four or five generations, although in some cases less, that have been trained to substitute their pursuit of well-being with the pursuit of wealth, buying stuff that we think will make us feel better, which it may do, for a second, until it makes us feel worse.

The other good news is that mass-consumerism has been harshly criticized from all corners of the planet since it gained its overwhelming currency. Even from within the heart of western capitalism, we have always felt there was something wrong with it. Materialism is a bad thing; we are told again and again. You can't buy happiness. Would it be possible to return to something that may have existed before consumerist hell broke loose? Of course, history is much more impervious and compli-cated than a simple before and after, a better or worse. Before mass-consumerism, there was mostly mass-poverty, and so we are tempted to believe that capitalism has caused both our wealth and our well-being.[3] Contrary to what it might seem like, this essay is not an attempt at an all-encompassing philos-ophy on consumerism or materialism or socio-economic in-equality. It is an attempt to point at some hopeful nuances in a time where we may feel like we have no alternative to the growth ideology of capitalism that is propelling us towards our very own extinction. It is an effort to put this apocalyptic ideology into a perspective that does include the alternatives, which are right there for us to pick up and take on.

Ready-to-Waste
versus
Conservative Consumption

And so, we are back at the simple urge to consume conserva-tively and to conserve what we already have. Within fashion this idea has become a no-brainer, yet it is one that proves difficult to combine with our thirst for the *new*. The fashion industry is an enormous two-headed snake, which on one side is churning out "ready-to-waste" rather than "ready-to-wear" collections at lightning speed, and on the other side is scratching its head

Good Materialism

looking for ethical alternatives to the polluting and exploitative hyperobject that it has become.[4] From H&M investing a considerable amount into organic cotton, to an increasing popularity of vintage and second-hand clothing, mainly because there is *just so damn much* of it. What everyone and everything keeps ignoring, is that we (that is us, privileged people of the world, you know who you are) need to work towards a degrowth scenario. That is progress by looking back, behind us. We don't need more; we need less stuff. With every step we take we need to check what we leave behind and ensure we take care of it. This is a plea for a new type of conservatism: that of conservative consumption. We need to conserve what we have, and progress by caring for it. It is time for a new materialism, a Good Materialism. A materialism that judges us not by newness but by the age of our stuff. Because to consume extravagantly in times of climate crisis is worse than hedonistic, it is suicidal.

Marjanne Van Helvert

1

Brown, M. (2014). *CC41 Utility Clothing.*
Kent: Sabrestorm Publishing.

2

See also: Helvert, MJ van. "Good
Design for Everyone: Scarcity, Equality,
and Utility in the Second World War".
In: Helvert, MJ van (ed.). (2016). *The
Responsible Object: A History of Design
Ideology for the Future.* Amsterdam: Valiz
Publishers.

3

Unless you go back further before the
Industrial to the Agricultural Revolution
and are a fan of Jean-Jacques Rousseau
and/or Yuval Harari, who believe humans
were lost ever since we left our hunter-
gatherer lifestyles behind.

4

I refer here to the concept "hyperobject"
as explained by Timothy Morton.
A hyperobject, according to him, is
something that is so enormous and so
much spread out over time and space,
that we can never grasp or understand
it in its entirety, such as climate change,
or radioactive waste. The global fashion
industry can also be understood as a
hyperobject.

fig. 1

11   Good Materialism

fig. 2

Marjanne Van Helvert

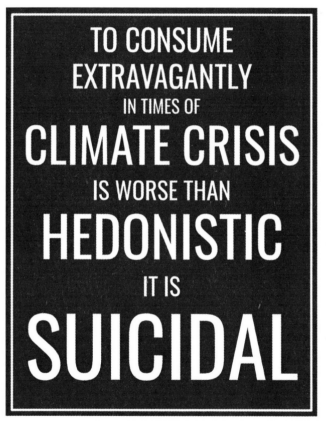

fig. 3

Queerness ≠ conservative(ness)

Yamuna Forzani

No racism
No sexism
No homophobia
No transphobia
No xenophobia
No ableism
No ageism
No classism
No fatphobia
No hate
Be aware of the energy you bring into the space

When I think of the word conservative, I always think of something that is very restrained: a stiff upper lip, holding yourself back, suppressing feelings and emotions. Yet I can't relate to any of these visions. As a 'flower child' of hippie parents that fell in love on the beaches of Goa in the 1980s, I have been exposed to alternative philosophies and ways of living from a young age and can therefore safely say that there is nothing conservative about me.

I am originally from the UK and moved to The Netherlands in 2012, due to the raising of tuition fees for universities – from £3,000 to £9,000 per year – by Conservative Prime Minister David Cameron. At the time I had been actively involved in the student riots and protests surrounding the fees and feeling deflated and disappointed that the protests hadn't changed anything, I decided to move to The Netherlands to study Fashion and Textiles at the Royal Academy of Art in The Hague and have been living and working here ever since.

My position in the design field

Before calling myself an artist or designer, I would say that I am first and foremost a queer activist. My form of activism is staying true to feminist ideologies, environmental practices, and human rights politics in all areas of my life, especially my creative practice. I graduated from art school four years ago from the fashion and textile department and since then, I have been using my colourful vibrant clothing and textile installations to make

positive, anarchistic statements to celebrate my community. My aim is always to create safe spaces and be an advocate for the LGBTQ+ community. I want to create a queer utopia away from the conservative, heteronormative ideals of society.

I am a part of the International Ballroom scene, an underground community that was birthed by Harlem's marginalised queer, black and Latinx folks in the 1980s. During this period, being a person of colour in society was very difficult – as it still is – and identifying as gay or trans made life almost impossible – as, again, it still is. Balls are therefore a safe haven for competition where members of the scene battle in different categories for trophies. The community grew from struggle, providing the context not only for performance and costume design, but for cultural commentary, friendship, and AIDS awareness. It is a space to explore gender and sexuality within a community where such freedoms can be fostered and celebrated.

Balls are famous in mainstream culture for the performance category 'Voguing'. Voguing is a certain dance to music that imitates the characteristic poses struck by a model on a catwalk and/or in a fashion magazine. Today, the ballroom scene is becoming more popular thanks to shows such as POSE on Netflix, My House on VICE and Legendary Max on HBO. In Europe, we have an established ballroom scene with members representing all different houses, from all different backgrounds, genders, sexualities.

I discovered the scene back in 2016, when a member of the Kiki House of Angels started voguing at a video casting that I had organized. I was so excited and shocked, especially as I had been obsessed with the film 'Paris is Burning' as a kid. Yet despite this I hadn't known that the ballroom scene existed in The Netherlands or even Europe. After this initial moment of realisation, I was hooked! The first ball I ever attended was in 2016 in Rotterdam and I remember sweating the whole time, realising that this is the exact thing I have been looking for my entire life. The room was so full of love and this alone was so incredible and truly inspiring. Bodies of all different shapes, sizes, sexualities, genders, ethnicities being celebrated and empowered moved me so deeply.

After having discovered the ballroom scene, I became a member of the Kiki House of Angels in the Netherlands and

19   *Yamuna Forzani*

an international member of New York's House of Comme des Garcons. I compete in the fashion categories at the ball including: Best Dressed, where you are judged on your outfit styling; Designers Delight, a fashion design category where one is judged on the design and skills of finishing a garment; and Bizarre – my favourite category to compete in. In Bizarre, you have to make an outfit that is more like an installation on the body made out of unconventional materials. It has to be other-worldly and strange. I like this category the most as it allows me to show off my quirky, outrageous creativity using found, and mostly recycled materials. Usually, the themes are very extrav-agant and strange, for example: "An acid trip on the Vegas strip". Walking Balls really helps me in my professional practice as it's a place where I can play and flirt with new ideas and experiment freely.

Despite the scene still being considered somewhat underground, it is growing, and I want to encourage its growth as I believe so many queer BIPOC can benefit from this wonderful utopian world of creativity and free expression that this culture houses. Fuelled by my personal, professional and political views, I try to do so respectfully.

Inventing the alternative

At this time of writing, I have been navigating my way profes-sionally since graduation when I discovered I really do not want to be part of the fashion industry – at least not in the traditional sense. I had witnessed first-hand the toxic environment it can be, with its elitism that does not relate to or embody my ethics at all. This is why I am so motivated to invent an alternative. I feel that the concept of a classic fashion show and fashion collec-tion is now almost outdated. So, with this in mind I created the concept of 'The Utopia Ball x Fashion Show'.

The Utopia Ball x Fashion show is an event platform I created as I've never seen such a combination before of a fash-ion show and a ball. This combination makes so much sense to me as there are so many designers in the scene who deserve to be in the spotlight. I named this platform the Utopia Ball because of the idea of a 'Utopia' creating a better world, a con-

cept that is the biggest motivation in my practice. So far, the ball is annual but we have had to postpone the Utopia Ball 2020 due to the virus, therefore the next Utopia Ball will be held in 2021. The last edition of the Utopia Ball x Fashion show was in September 2019 and its theme was The New Paradise. The theme focused on sustainability and encouraged participants to make outfits from recycled materials and rubbish. I considered it important to bring such environmental consciousness into the ball setting.

Despite the changing themes, what remains highly important in organizing all of these balls is that community comes first. Period. Therefore, in every one of the Balls I involve the communities surrounding them from start to finish. I break down any upending traditional hierarchies ruling in the fashion industry by working together with my peers and models directly – to ensure no interference from agencies in any sort of way. For example, for the last edition of Utopia Ball I made space for other designers to show their work alongside my own. I also had the trophies made and designed by a queer local artist, Hannah Mulqueen, who used recycled plexiglass and wood to craft 30 trophies for the winners of each ballroom category. I deem it highly important to keep on making space and creating a platform where no one is left behind or feels left out.

How to organize a queer inclusive event 101

Based upon my own experience and ethics, and what the scene has brought me both personally and professionally, I wish to take this opportunity to spread some queer knowledge in the form of a 101 on organizing a queer-inclusive event. This 101 is not only useful for people who wish to organize queer-inclusive events but any event organizer out there who wishes to make a change, whether within or outside of the world of (fashion) design.

Intentional Spaces
When organizing a queer-inclusive event it is important to know that queer people feel safe and seen. To do this, you need to design an event with the intention to centre

and prioritise queer womxn, non-binary and trans folk of colour. There are many ways of achieving this. To start with I like to have discounted tickets available for the audience I am prioritizing whilst allies who want to support pay the full price. For example, for the last ball I organized the ticket pricing was as follows:

Members of the scene who are walking the ball   *5€*
Womxn, non-binary and trans folk of colour guests *7,50€*
Ally guests   *12,50€*

I also made a manifesto wall hanging behind the ticket booth for when people came inside to remind them that we have zero tolerance for harassment or prejudice of any kind. The manifesto was inspired by the stage décor at AfroPunk festival. That same manifesto can be read at the beginning of this essay and may serve as a friendly reminder for the space I inhabit through this essay and within this book as well. I want people to understand that they are safe and to remind anyone that there will be no tolerance for hate speech.

Accessibility
Accessibility is so important. Especially when organizing a queer-inclusive event. It's necessary to think about wheelchair accessibility, being close to public transport, and adequate seating and of course gender-neutral bathrooms. Also, not to have strobe lights. It is also important to have a taxi fund: a donation box at the entrance where allies and guests can put money in to ensure that queer womxn, non-binary and trans folk of colour who need / request it can get home safely. Not only is it important, it is necessary to implement such acts of care.

Safe Space
It's crucial to make it clear that people can come to the organisers, members of staff or volunteers when feeling unsafe. To make this clear you can make an announcement at the beginning of the event and also on social media. It is useful to have the members of staff wearing

something that is clearly recognizable; a t-shirt or a badge, for example.

Photography

When arranging event photography for your queer-inclusive gathering, it is necessary to hire a queer photographer and ensure they understand the importance of asking for consent first. At the balls I organize and have attended certain categories such as 'sex siren' or 'body' – in which people are particularly revealing themselves– we usually create a Google Drive folder and send it to the participants after, rather than posting the photos onto social media channels. That being said, it's also important that anyone else coming in to take photographs should ask for consent. The aim is to create a safe space for people to feel free.

The personal = professional = political

With this essay, I wish to show the interconnectivity of the personal and the political through the professional. As we all know, the personal is political. In my case, and for so many others, the personal is professional is political. The one seeps through the other and vice versa, especially for queer folks trying to navigate their way within a society that upholds conservative and heteronormative ideals, structures and systems.

Going back to where I started this essay with, I think again of the word conservative and how I can(not) relate. Whether it concerns the personal, the professional, or the political, I really do feel that queerness is the opposite of conservative(ness). It is hard to imagine one being a queer activist whilst being highly conservative at the same time – the one almost immediately eliminates the other. In identifying as queer, does one automatically identify as anti-conservative? And the other way around? These are questions I wish to leave here for your consideration. In the meantime, in staying true to my activism in all areas of life and in creating my queer utopia away from the conservative heteronormative ideals of society, I will keep on advocating for the LGBTQ+ community, celebration, and positivity altogether.

23   Yamuna Forzani

fig. 1

Queerness ≠ conservative(ness)

fig. 2

Yamuna Forzani

fig. 3

Queerness ≠ conservative(ness)

fig. 1
Utopia ball by David Morrison

fig. 2
fashion show Trafalgar square
photography by David Morrison

fig. 3
Utopia ball by Celine

Yamuna Forzani

A fashionable riddle

Studio PMS

The new decennium could not have started off more dramatically than with a global pandemic. After being raised in a society where growth, change and pioneering formed the pillars of our economy, we are now at the mercy of a physical and mental standstill. We therefore took this essay as an opportunity to discuss this contradiction between progressing and standing still, also known as conservatism and progressivism.

A fear of repetition

We live in a time where new influences are as fleeting as our most recent Tinder dates. The word *innovation* has been used tirelessly by many a start-up or undefinable agency, which makes the word itself appear as cliché, dusty and obsolete. Our society's wish for continuous change encourages us to do something new, time and time again. Go travel somewhere! Experience new things! Go on an adventure! Push your boundaries! When we experience something new, our consciousness runs at full capacity. Therefore, many of our firsts make it into the "wall of fame" of our memory, with renewal and innovation lying at the core of our personal and professional mantras: *renew, innovate, repeat*. We then tend to apologize for repetition, even though it is repetition itself that adds value to innovation. Repetition is often mistaken for a lack of creativity and inspiration. For many designers repetition can feel like plagiarism – not only repetition of snippets of others' ideas, but also the repetition of our own ideas or findings. All of which can feel as though we are stuck in the creative process.

The fear of stagnation is tremendous, especially within the ever-changing landscape of the creative industries. And to be honest, the fear of losing relevance is a legitimate one. Throughout history, the work or vision of many prominent figures has been denounced as outdated. Take Gabrielle "Coco" Chanel, for example. In the 1920s, she helped introduce sporty materials, a more breathable silhouette and (for that period) debatable skirt lengths within women's fashion. Ever since, the fashion house of Coco Chanel has been on the march again and again – even literally 'on the march' when Karl Lagerfeld took on the role of head designer – yet never has it conveyed such a strong or

leading statement since its conception. In a way, you could wonder whether innovation is something you can continuously pursue. Is the idea of continuous innovation not inherently a conservative ideology? After all, by renewing again and again, the true message behind an innovative idea hardly resonates due to its fleetingness.

It is precisely this urge or need for continuous innovation that appears to be one of the biggest pitfalls of fashion and its highly polluting industry. Of all the clothing items for sale at the larger fashion retailers' shops – those who produce new collections every two weeks – the majority will never be sold. In order to maintain a highly commercialized fashion system, overproduction is considered a necessary by-product of the current system. However, there is a group of kindred spirits who wish to move away from such an exploitative system and who see possibilities in enhancing and progressing within the fashion industry. We at Studio PMS, for example, believe that digitizing the process of designing, sampling and fitting before a product goes into actual, physical production is pivotal. Not only could digitalization make the sampling-process more practical and sustainable, it could also reduce overproduction and make way for a more personalized system in which there is more room for quality and conscious consumption and a re-appreciation for the craft behind fashion can commence. However, this leads us to question whether our need for the re-appreciating of craft is not a conservative idea(l)? Take, for example, the research question we were occupied with during our studio's early days: "How can we preserve tactility within the digital world?" – although this particular question came from an ideological need to change the current fashion system for the better, the verb to *preserve* is literally used within it.

To partly answer the question whether our need for re-appreciating craft within the fashion system is indeed a conservative ideal: it might just be. In our opinion, conservatism is an appreciation of the past *and* a fear of the unknown (e.g. change) whilst innovation encapsulates a fear of repetition *and* a need for change and/or betterment. In a way, both conservatism and innovation are fuelled by hopes as much as fears. For us, it is important not to be led nor frightened by fear but to instead ask questions and look at the matter as objectively as possible.

We hereby not only look at our own practice, but also at other practices within and beyond the fashion industry. It is important to be able to define where the fears that cause these conservative ideologies come from; and only then will we be able to create an accurate image of what is at stake within our industry and why change within it takes such tremendous efforts.

Studio PMS's vision did not necessarily emerge from an urge to be innovative; we simply did not want to partake in the fashion industry's systems that awaited us at the end of our fashion design studies and at the beginning of our professional careers. For us, a more fitting and obvious reaction was to dive into the fashion world and all its challenges uninhibited and with a healthy dose of enthusiasm. Being a small studio, we realize that these ideals – and thereby our different take on the design process – are easier said and done by us than, for example, big multinationals that have a lot of financial responsibility and that would need to undergo huge changes and face the consequences that these would cause. However, if we think from a space where there is room for experiment, we can investigate new business models that show us how to deal with the fashion industry and its crooked systems in a different manner. Perhaps our naivety is exactly what makes us take the road unknown, a road mostly considered impassable by those more experienced.

An appreciation of the past

Being big enthusiasts of the lively imaginative force that lives and breathes within fashion, we tend to become nostalgic from time to time. And yet, when feeling such nostalgia, we are fearful of making things that are born from our own fascination only, without taking into account possible negative consequences. For us, this is one of the main motivations in actively searching for innovation. However, the fact that we search for innovative ways to change the fashion industry does not necessarily mean we never deal with conservative thoughts and needs. To appreciate the past suggests an appreciation of things long gone or of things at stake. Conservatism – the need to conserve what has been – is inextricably bound with change and a fear for that change. To put it differently; if there would be nothing to lose

there would be nothing to hold onto altogether, right? Fear is necessary for animals to survive within the natural world, yet we humans tend to detach from it by trying to consciously suppress fear(ful thoughts).

Fashion used to be visually dictated by the lucky few who had the so-called *fingerspitzengefühle* and who were able to translate outstanding and advanced ideals into physical garments and outfits. Designers would shed their light on ideas about beauty, lifestyle, and aesthetics through their creations. Paul Poiret, Elsa Schiaparelli, and Cristobal Balenciaga are only a few examples of leading figures within the fashion industry whose ideas and sense of style were recklessly copied by others. One of the consequences being that individuals were less likely to critically assess whether the garment actually 'fitted' them or not.

We now live in an era in which we have unlimited access to an endless amount of information and knowledge. This means there is less need for us to fall back on fashion shown on the catwalk and in magazines alone in order to know what the newest trends are. In a way, this has stimulated the rise of consumer individualism – who still wants to be told what (not) to wear this season? We prefer to surround ourselves with like-minded spirits who cherish and appreciate the whimsical. Nowadays, consciousness as well as selectiveness are being encouraged within the fashion scene. This makes for fashion designers to take on a different role to before. Fashion no longer exists only through the lens of a select group of designers, but instead captures the zeitgeist of a society at large. Inspiration no longer is a one-way traffic road, but a continuous cross-pollination of social references. As a result, inspiration for fashion is sought after in the mundane, like the utility trend that emerged from a study into traditional workwear uniforms. Our online environment including social media has accelerated everything fashion, making for a growth of variation both in designs and designers.

Within the industry, change is most likely paired with a revert to production methods from the past. Five years ago, futurist / trend forecaster Lidewij Edelkoort suggested in a manifesto that the concept of fashion was long gone. According to Edelkoort it is precisely the love for clothing that needs to return. Quite the contradiction when you think of the idea behind and definition of a futurist / trend forecaster. And so, you see: our

sometimes-conservative ideas can come across as contemporary and relevant. Designers like to be in control of what is happening now, to be a part of the change in order to prevent themselves from lagging behind – all under the guise of change and innovation. Yet in amongst such change and progression we must not forget to conserve the things that are worth bringing into the future.

Studio PMS has existed for two years now and we have become more confident in our *raison d'être* – our right to exist – within the fashion industry. We experience trust within our collaborations. Our clients bring requests that build upon our earlier work which, for them, guarantees a certain amount of quality and speed in what we are able to deliver. In search of balance between artistic and financial freedom as independent, self-employed designers, we also tend to find ourselves in a repetitive loop – something we for so long resisted against. Take for example the animations we at Studio PMS make for our projects. The first animations for 'In Pursuit of Tactility' emerged from the need to breathe virtual life into a digital collection of fabrics and materials that had already been created two years ago. By making the 3D models move within the film, we were able to create and generate a sense of reality and tactility. The idea behind the project was to show the fashion industry that a digital collection is able to convey the feelings and experiences that fashion, clothing and fabric are able to convey in the corporeal world.

After completing the project, we received an enormous number of requests for digital fashion shoots and animations. To be able to work with clients such as Nike, Adidas and Burberry at such an early moment in our careers was amazing. And still, these clients offer us a consistent amount of commissions. With such gained traction, comes further considerations, such as what then remains of our original ethos from which the innovative idea has sprouted? Should we hold onto that one innovative and commercially attractive idea, or will it lose its innovative value through commercialization? This is something we ask ourselves frequently and to which we do not have the answer yet. Furthermore, it is quite the challenge to find partners who pursue the same ideals as we do. If our differences are purely about taste or aesthetics then this could make for an inter-

esting boost to the project at hand. However, if it concerns a difference in vision towards the fashion industry, then it becomes harder for us to stomach. Nevertheless, we think that collaborating with brands that do not always prioritize sustainability and innovation as much as we do could still cause a chain reaction within the fashion industry at large. And for us, each tiny step towards a slow revolution is more than worth it.

A conservative thought often references an example from the past in which something was experienced to be 'better', or it references a custom that is still considered valuable today. For us, there is no need for completely new beginnings. We do not foresee a surrealistic sci-fi future. Nor a world in which we float around in our jet skis wearing holographic necklaces. We believe that the innovative techniques we investigate should be able to integrate in today's fashion industry. To be able to show and to shed light on the possibility of combining conservation and innovation, we must make clear the need for restructuring and integration within the industry. If we do so, the fear for change will slowly become irrelevant and there will be room for making new connections. Conserving the important innovations from the past whilst innovating in the present. How great is that?

Time for time

The fashion industry as we know it today must change – that is a fact. Overproduction still triumphs within the bigger fashion brands. By maintaining this hierarchical structure within the fashion industry only a select few have access to the system and its challenges, thereby warding off others that come into play. The urge for Studio PMS to change the industry from within does not necessarily mean all of its current aspects, knowledge and customs should be rigorously thrown away. We used innovation as a tool to conserve. Conservatism can therefore be understood as a simple appreciation for prior innovations. To take us, for example, we do not believe in an industry where production and consumption happen merely digitally.

Both progressivism and conservatism are a hotbed of hopes as well as fears. In both circumstances it is the fear to lose. For innovation it is the fear to lose opportunity. Opportunities

are the more fun and exciting things in life: when you take an opportunity and have an impact, it can cause a sense of invincibility. Opportunities are an ode to curiosity. For conservatism, however, it is the fear of losing what *was* – that which feels familiar, that which fulfils expectations, and that which brings balance.

The beauty and duality of this discussion is that the two are intrinsically linked to one another. To conserve is to make way for progression. To innovate is to make variations of all that already exists. That which distinguishes them is also that which connects them, and we should reflect more on a process of combining them. Can we do better? Or is it already better? And is doing things *otherwise* altogether "better"? We try to find a meticulous balance in this. If it were up to us, there is one thing we would like to give ourselves and others in order to establish a more reflective state of mind within the fashion industry: **time.** Whether it is time to look forward or time to look back. Either way, we have ample time in the very present to do so.

A fashionable riddle

fig. 1

fig. 2

A fashionable riddle

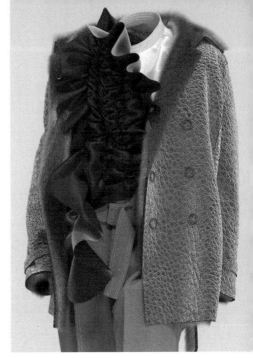

fig. 3

fig. 1–3   courtesy of the author

Studio PMS